10 Minutes a Day to Reading Success

activities and skill builders to help your kindergartner learn to love reading

Houghton Mifflin Company
Boston   New York   1998

Product Development: Editorial Options, Inc.
Project Editor: Gari Fairweather
Designer: Lynne Torrey

Illustrations by Shirley Beckes
Pencil page spot art previously published in Houghton Mifflin's *Phonics, Books 1-5*, copyright (c)
1997 by Houghton Mifflin Company. Pencil page art also by: Liz Callen, Susan Jaeckel, Ron Lehew,
Ed Parker, Lou Vaccaro, Joe Veno

For information about permission to reproduce selections from this book, write to Permissions,
Houghton Mifflin Company, 215 Park Avenue South, New York, New York, 10003.

ISBN 0-395-90152-9

Printed in the United States of America

DOC 10 9 8 7 6 5 4 3 2 1

Table of Contents

Introduction..5

Chapter 1: Color My World   7–22

Chapter Note 8
Color Everywhere...................9
Color Magic 10
Colorful Fruits....................11
A Color Rhyme Card 12
Color-Rhyme Match 13
Alphabet Fun......................14

My Own Alphabet.................15
Chain of Letters..................16
ABC Connect-the-Dots 17
Letter Memory Game 18
Letter Cards.......................19
Books to Share....................20
My Story: A Color Rhyme........21

Chapter 2: Count with Me   23–40

Chapter Note 24
How Many? How Many? 25
A Number Snake...................26
Count It Out!......................27
Domino Play 28
Domino Cards......................29
A Counting Rhyme 30
Rhyme a Number 31

Make a Counting Book 32
Beginning Sounds 33
Kitchen Art 34
M is for Monkey 35
Beginning Sound Dictionary 36
S is for Seven.....................37
Books to Share 38
My Story: My Counting Rhyme ...39

Chapter 3: Animal Fair   41–58

Chapter Note.......................42
Animal Safari......................43
Animal Posters....................44
Sort It Out!........................45
My Very Own Pet Rock 46
D is for Dog........................47
Put Me in the Zoo 48
H is for Hippo 49
Kitchen Critters 50

B is for Bug 51
Make a Songbook 52
G is for Goat 53
Word Wheels.......................54
Picture-Word Matchup 55
Look at all the things I can do! ...56
Books to Share 57
My Story: What Did It Say?......58

Chapter 4: Friends and Family 59–76

Chapter Note 60

My Family Is Special 61

Friends and Family Tree 62

Friends and Family Leaves.........................63

A Book of Friends 64

F is for Family 65

A Family Breakfast 66

P is for Pig 67

Paper Presents...68

C is for Card 69

Fly a Friendship Kite 70

K is for Kite 71

Games to Play 72

Race Home 73

Books to Share 74

My Story: My Friends and Family 75

Chapter 5: The Way I Feel 77–94

Chapter Note 78

Sing a Song 79

What's in a Face? 80

Happy or Sad? 81

A Week of Feelings...................................82

W is for Week 83

My Five Senses 84

L is for Lion 85

Taste Test 86

T is for Taste 87

Busy Hands 88

N is for Nap 89

Sliding Words...90

Two Sliding Words 91

Books to Share 92

My Story: How I Feel 93

Chapter 6: Rhyme Me a Story 95–112

Chapter Note 96

Favorite Rhymes 97

Picture This! 98

A Picture Poem..99

Rhymes for Outside Fun 100

J is for Jump 101

Comic Strip Rhymes.................................102

R is for Rabbit 103

This Is the Way... 104

Y is for Yellow 105

Act Out a Rhyme 106

V is for Vase..107

Flip Books 108

Flip Book Patterns 109

Look at all the things I can do! 110

Books to Share 111

My Story: A Little Rhyme 112

Introduction

Getting Started

Your child is off to kindergarten! You're probably wondering what you can do to help your child succeed in school. If you're like most of today's busy adults, you're juggling several projects at a time and looking to focus on those things that will *really* be helpful.

How can you reinforce what your child is learning in school? One way is to let your child see you reading. When you read, your child sees that reading is a worthwhile activity. Another way is to read with your child. When you share a book, your child not only has a chance to practice his or her reading skills but also to feel close to you. You can also share many different kinds of activities that promote literacy and are fun to do. That's where this book comes in.

Using *10 Minutes a Day to Reading Success*

This book contains activities you and your child can do together to reinforce concepts and skills being taught in school. Some can be completed in as little as ten minutes. Others are a bit more involved. There is no correct time limit for completing an activity, however, since each child works at his or her own pace. Look for these icons as a general guide to the amount of time an activity might take:

 estimates the minutes required for an activity

 denotes activities requiring more than half an hour

 identifies activities centered in the kitchen

You'll find that activities with the kitchen icon make use of materials and staples found in your kitchen. Many of the other projects require materials readily found in most homes, such as crayons, markers, glue, scissors, paper, and index cards. Still other activities, like our pencil pages, invite your child to color and write in the book. Some of these pages can be completed independently, so if you need to step away for a minute, your child can continue without you.

You'll notice that the book is divided into thematic chapters designed to help your child acquire vocabulary and expand his or her knowledge base. Each chapter begins with a brief note to you that identifies the reading skills practiced in the chapter's activities. Look also for these icons, which provide information for parents, teachers, and other adults.

 Note explains a reading skill or suggests ways in which to complete an activity.

 Helping Hand provides tips for an activity, suggests alternative materials, or provides information of interest.

 More Ideas offers suggestions for other projects or ways to expand an especially enjoyable activity.

Each chapter includes a list of theme-related books you can share with your child. (You may want to gather these books early on, so you can enjoy them throughout a chapter.) At the end of each chapter is a story your child can read independently or withyour help.

Feel free to photocopy or to cut up the pages. You can also use our pencil pages more than once. You might use them at the beginning of a chapter to determine how much your child already knows or use them at the end to find out how much your child has learned. Keep track of the activities your child completes by coloring in the circle at the bottom of each page.

About Learning to Read
Learning to read is a process that takes time, practice, and some patience, and most reading skills need not be taught in a lockstep fashion. Some research suggests that a child should learn to say the ABC's and to identify alphabet letters before learning letter-sound correspondences. However, if your child knows some of the letters of the alphabet, he or she may be ready to learn the sounds of these letters (phonics) before learning the names of other letters. Research also demonstrates the importance of focusing on the different sounds in a word (phonemic awareness) and distinguishing between words based on those different sounds. This ability is an important predictor of success in learning to read.

Phonemic awareness works hand-in-hand with phonics to help beginning readers decode words. Phonics activities help a child to match spoken sounds and written letters. For instance, young children will learn to associate beginning sounds (such as the /b/ sound at the beginning of *bat*) and written letters (such as *b*). Children will also learn about rhyming words and their common parts (such as the *-at* in *bat*, *cat*, *mat*, and *sat*). Saying nursery rhymes with your child and naming the words that rhyme will help your child to focus on these word parts. Saying tongue-twisters with your child will help him or her to focus on the beginning sounds.

The order in which you complete the activities in this book is up to you. You can work through one chapter, and then move on to the next. Or, you might skip around, choosing activities that appeal to your child. (Note: If your child's school uses Houghton Mifflin's reading/language arts program INVITATIONS TO LITERACY, there is a direct correspondence between the sequence of skills presented in that program and the sequence of the skills presented in this book.)

We hope you and your child will have fun. We know that finding time to do one more thing in a busy day is never easy. But by making the most of the time you do have—even ten minutes a day—you can make a big difference in your child's attitude toward reading!

CHAPTER 1

Color My World

Roses Are Red

Roses are red.

Violets are blue.

Sugar is sweet,

And so are you!

A Note About Color My World

One of the first ways in which children begin to describe and define their world is through color. In *Color My World*, youngsters can explore the concept of color and practice color words through a variety of activities as they practice the alphabet and these skills:

ALPHABET LETTERS: Beginning kindergartners spend a lot of school time learning the alphabet. The pages here will reinforce these skills, as your child practices reciting the alphabet, naming the individual letters, and matching the capital and lowercase forms of letters.

PHONEMIC AWARENESS/RHYMING WORDS: In preparation for associating sounds with letters, your child will learn to listen for ways in which words are similar and different. This chapter focuses on listening for and producing rhyming words.

NOTING DETAILS: In most picture books, the words tell only part of the story; the pictures tell the other part. Kindergartners are learning to look for details in a story's pictures—details that are important to the story line.

SEQUENCE: Children soon learn that some things follow a special order. A story, for example, has a beginning, a middle, and an end. Directions have steps with words like *first, next,* and *last.* Here, your child can begin to practice sequence through the use of the alphabet.

In addition to the above skills, kindergartners begin to learn important reading strategies. One such strategy is *making predictions,* or trying to figure out what a book will be about, based on its title and cover illustration. While reading a book together, encourage your child to pause and predict what might happen next. Then read on to find out how close he or she came.

Introduce *Color My World* by reading the traditional verse on page 7. Ask your youngster to name the colors mentioned in the rhyme; then encourage him or her to color the panda and flowers. Then read the rhyme again and ask your child to listen for the rhyming words.

Color Everywhere

Take a look around you. Where can you find colors? Colors are inside and outside, on the ground and in the air. Colors, you might say, are everywhere.

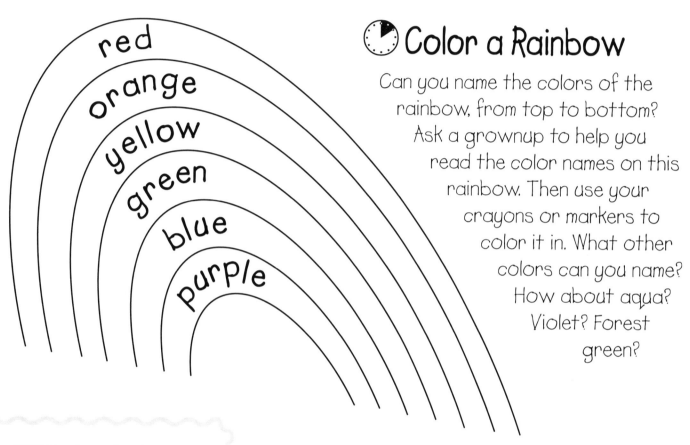

red
orange
yellow
green
blue
purple

Color a Rainbow

Can you name the colors of the rainbow, from top to bottom? Ask a grownup to help you read the color names on this rainbow. Then use your crayons or markers to color it in. What other colors can you name? How about aqua? Violet? Forest green?

Naming colors is a concept your child can practice anywhere and any time. Help your child master the basic colors early on.

Point out color words on crayons, and encourage your child to "read" the color of each crayon before using it. Provide extra practice with color word cards. Write each color name on an index card, using a crayon or marker of that color. Your child can use the color word cards to label differently colored items in your home.

Color Hunt

What colors can you find in your home? Go on a color hunt to find out. Try to find something for each color of the rainbow. If you want, take your color hunt outside. Flowers and autumn leaves come in many different colors.

Did you find at least one thing for each color of the rainbow? Draw pictures to show some of the things you found.

Color Magic

Have you ever mixed two colors together? Have you ever taken a color apart? Try these two activities, and see what happens!

Mixing Colors Together

You can mix colors by using paper cups, water, and food coloring. Here's what you do:

- Put a little water in a paper cup.

- Add two drops of red food coloring to the water and two drops of yellow food coloring.

What color do red and yellow make when you mix them? Draw a picture to show what happens. What happens when you mix red and blue or when you mix blue and yellow?

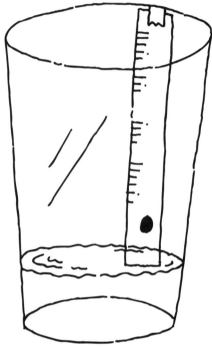

Taking Colors Apart

To take a color apart, try this:

- Cut a coffee filter into strips.

- With a black or brown marker, put a dot at one end of the strip.

- Tape the strip to the inside of a glass.

- Add water so that just the end of the strip is in the water.

- Watch what happens. Do you see the water rising up the strip? What happens when the dot gets wet? Draw pictures to show it.

Try this project with other marker colors, too!

You can use watercolors instead of food coloring and paper towels instead of coffee filters in these activities.

Help your child note details by asking questions as you do the activities. Your child may also dictate sentences about the details included in his or her drawings.

Colorful Fruits

Read the color words and color each crayon and fruit. Use fruits like these to make a tasty salad!

red

yellow

green

blue

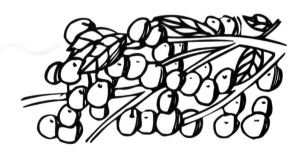

Picture Names: *strawberry, banana, grapes, blueberries*

A Color Rhyme Card

Roses are red.
Daisies are yellow.
Grandpa Joe is a very nice fellow.

Do you like to draw pictures for your family? Do you ever tell people how special they are? If so, you'll like making a color rhyme card.

Make a Rhyme

Look at the rhyme on page 7 and read it again. Do you see how the color **blue** rhymes with **you**? Think of more color rhymes to make new messages for "Roses Are Red."

Make a Card

Once you have a rhyme you like, you're ready to make the card. Here's how:

1) To make the card, fold a piece of paper in half so it opens and closes like a book.

2) Write the name of the person you'll give the card to on the outside of the card.

3) Ask a grownup to write the rhyme on the inside. Be sure to sign your name, too.

4) If you want, draw pictures on your card.

5) Give the card to your special someone.

A child hears and identifies rhymes before being able to produce them. If your child has trouble thinking of a rhyme, suggest a few possibilities for him or her to choose from.

After your child identifies the rhyming pairs on the following pencil page, take turns naming other rhyming words for each pair.

Color-Rhyme Match

Name the pictures.
When you find two pictures
that rhyme, color them.
Use a different color
for each rhyme.

Picture Names: *cat, hat, mouse, boat, jar, car, house, coat*

Alphabet Fun

Can you think of different ways to practice the alphabet? How about writing it? Here are two ideas you can try.

 I Know My ABC's

What song names all the letters of the alphabet? That's right! It's "The ABC Song."

Sing the song with a grownup. Then look at the next page. It shows all the letters of the alphabet. Sing the song again. This time, point to the letters as you sing.

🕐 Rainbow Writing

Now that you can sing the alphabet, try to write all of its letters. Take out crayons to match the colors of the rainbow. Then use the crayons to trace each letter on the pencil page. Here are some ideas:

- Name each letter as you trace it.
- Use a different color for each letter. Then repeat the colors.
- Trace the capital letters first. Then go back and trace the lowercase letters.
- Sing "The ABC Song" as you practice writing.

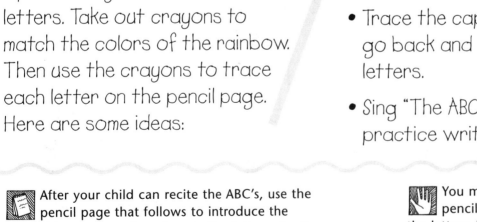

After your child can recite the ABC's, use the pencil page that follows to introduce the printed letters. Introduce four to five letters at a time, practicing these letters until your child can write them and match their capital and lowercase forms.

You may wish to copy the following pencil page before your child traces the letters. Your child can then cut apart the finished page to make an alphabet strip for his or her room.

My Own Alphabet

Alphabet letters have a certain order. Say the ABC's as you trace the letters. What letter does your name begin with?

✂

Aa — Bb — Cc — Dd

Paste second row here.

Ee — Ff — Gg — Hh — Ii

Paste third row here.

Jj — Kk — Ll — Mm

Paste fourth row here.

Nn — Oo — Pp — Qq

Paste fifth row here.

Rr — Ss — Tt — Uu — Vv

Paste sixth row here.

Ww — Xx — Yy — Zz

Chain of Letters

Here's a way to have fun with the alphabet and make a colorful paper chain for your room.

Get Ready...

Cut a sheet of construction paper into six long strips. Try to make all the strips the same size. Do this with four more sheets of paper. If you want, use different colors of paper. You'll also need paste.

Get Set...

Starting with **A**, write a letter on each strip. You can write just one letter (**A**) or both the capital letter and the lowercase letter (**Aa**). The alphabet on page 15 can help you.

Paste!

Line up the paper strips in ABC order. To make the chain, do this:

1) Paste the ends of the **A** strip together to make a circle.

2) Put the **B** strip through the **A** circle, and paste the ends of the **B** strip together.

3) Add the **C** strip to the **B** circle in the same way.

4) Keep adding strips to finish the alphabet.

5) Hang your chain of letters in your room!

The pencil page that follows provides practice with ABC order. Your child might find it helpful to sing softly "The ABC Song" as he or she connects the dots.

Cutting, writing, and pasting are fine-motor activities that can be time-consuming and tiring for a child. You may wish to divide the activity into smaller tasks for your child: cutting the strips one day; writing the letters the next; and making the chain the next.

A B C
Connect-the-Dots

Watch as your child says the alphabet and connects the dots. If your child falters, say the alphabet together. If necessary, use the alphabet strip on page 15 to practice saying the letters in order.

Letter Memory Game

Here's a fun way to practice the alphabet and test your memory!

◑ Get Ready to Play

Choose six letters of the alphabet. Make a capital letter card and a lowercase letter card for each letter (See page 19).

How to Play

First, find someone to play "Letter Memory" with you.

1) Mix up the letter cards. Place them face down on a table in rows.

2) Take turns turning over two cards. Try to match a capital and lowercase letter, like **D** and **d**.

3) If you make a match, you have to name the letters to keep the cards. If you do not make a match, turn the cards back over.

4) The player with the most letter cards wins!

   Do you really want to test your memory? Try using more letter cards to play the game.

The pencil page that follows can be copied, pasted onto cardboard, and cut apart to make letter cards. Play the memory game with different sets of letters.

In addition to playing the memory game, your child can use the letter cards to practice ABC order. Or, you can make several sets of letter cards to spell out words and sentences.

Letter Cards

A	a	B	b	C	c	D	d
E	e	F	f	G	g	H	h
I	i	J	j	K	k	L	l
M	m	N	n	O	o	P	p
Q	q	R	r	S	s	T	t
U	u	V	v	W	w	X	x
Y	y	Z	z				

Books to Share

Books that feature the colors and the alphabet abound in libraries and bookstores. Here's a sampling of titles you and your child might enjoy together.

Mary Wore Her Red Dress and Henry Wore His Green Sneakers by Merle Peek (Clarion, 1985). Katy's animal friends come to her birthday party dressed in clothes of different colors.

Mouse Paint by Ellen Stoll Walsh (Harcourt, 1989). Three mice experiment with red, yellow, and blue paint. Share the book after "Color Magic" on page 10, and let your child predict what will happen.

Brown Bear, Brown Bear, What Do You See? by Bill Martin, Jr. (Holt, 1992). A series of animals answer the question, "What do you see?" in this color book.

One Red Rooster by Suzette Barbier (Houghton, 1992). A lively rhyming verse brings together colors, animals, numbers, and sounds in this counting book. Ask your child to note details in the pictures.

More books you might enjoy:

Colors by Pascale De Bourgoing (Scholastic, 1991). This book has see-through pages that change the color of the pictures.

Chicka Chicka Boom Boom by Bill Martin, Jr., and John Archambault (Simon, 1991). Follow the letters of the alphabet on a raucous romp up and down a tree.

David McPhail's Animals A to Z by David McPhail (Scholastic, 1989). Look beyond the animal in each picture to find other items that begin with the featured letter.

Planting a Rainbow by Lois Ehlert (Harcourt, 1988). A child learns about the colors of the rainbow while planting a garden of flowers.

*My Story Suggestions

With your child, read the title and look at the pictures on the next page. Ask your child to predict what the story will be about.

✱ On a first reading, help your child read the color words and pause for him or her to color the items appropriately. Then read the story again and ask your child to supply the color words.

✱ Invite your child to draw and write a color rhyme to complete the story.

A Color Rhyme

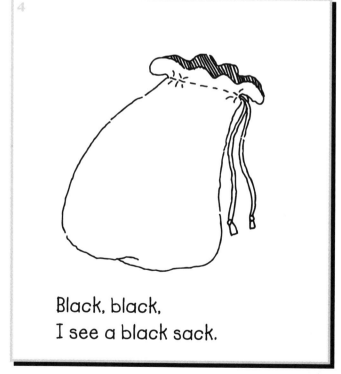

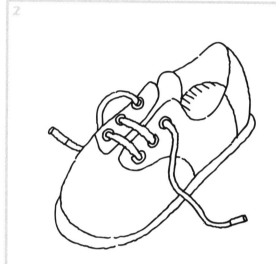

1

Red, red,
I see a red sled.

2

Blue, blue,
I see a blue shoe.

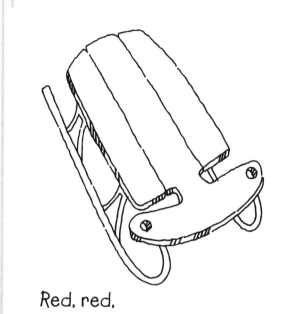

3

Pink, pink,
I see a pink sink.

4

Black, black,
I see a black sack.

* My Story

5

Green, green,
I see a green bean.

6

Brown, brown,
I see a brown clown.

7

_____, _____,

I see a _____ _____.

22

Count with Me

CHAPTER 2

One, Two, Three, Four, Five

One, two, three, four, five,

Once I caught a fish alive.

Six, seven, eight, nine, ten,

Then I let him go again.

A Note About Count with Me

Many children enter kindergarten able to recite the ABC's and the numbers *1* to *10*. It is in kindergarten, however, that most children begin to associate these letters and numbers with printed symbols. In *Count with Me*, youngsters will explore the numbers *1* to *10* while practicing these skills:

NUMBERS: Beginning kindergartners spend a lot of school time working with numbers. Your child will recite numbers, count items, and learn to recognize number symbols.

PHONEMIC AWARENESS: Before your child can learn to associate sounds with letters, he or she must learn to listen to the sounds in words. In this chapter, your child will practice listening for rhymes and beginning sounds.

PHONICS/INITIAL CONSONANTS: In addition to listening for beginning sounds, your child will learn two initial letter-sound correspondences, *m* and *s*.

SEQUENCE: In the last chapter, we practiced sequence through the use of the alphabet. Here, sequence will be explored through the use of numbers.

COMPARE/CONTRAST: Your child will explore not only the ways in which words are similar and different, but also the ways in which animals, people, and other items are similar and different. You can help your child by building on language skills that include adjectives such as *big, small, short, tall, soft, hard, fuzzy, smooth,* and so on.

In addition to making predictions (Chapter 1), another reading strategy your child will learn is *monitoring*. This strategy involves determining whether what is being read in a story makes sense and what to do if it doesn't. If something doesn't make sense as you read, your child will learn to apply "fix-up" strategies such as:

- reading again for information;
- reading ahead for information;
- looking at illustrations for help.

How Many? How Many?

Tell me quickly! How many eyes do you have? Fingers? Teeth? Oops, did you have to count your teeth? That's okay. Sometimes, you know how many without counting. Sometimes, you have to count.

Make a Guess

Now tell me quickly! Without counting, how many doors are in your home? How many windows? Make a guess, and write it down. What do you think—are there more windows or doors?

Check It Out

Now take a few minutes to count the doors and windows. If you want, keep track of your counting on a piece of paper. Did you check each room? Were you surprised by how many doors and windows you counted?

If you have time, think about other things you could count. Make a list with a grownup. First, try to guess how many for each thing. Then, count to find out.

Children recite numbers before making the one-to-one correspondence to count items. You can help your child by pointing to each item as it is counted.

Provide counting practice by playing "How Many?" as you go about chores or errands. Invite your child to guess and count the things you see—the stairs as you climb them, the items in the grocery cart, and so on.

A Number Snake

What can you do with some string and two cardboard tubes from paper towel rolls? Make a number snake, that's what!

 Get Ready

Ask a grownup to cut the tubes into two-inch wide sections. Count out ten sections. If you want, paint or color the sections with bright colors.

When the sections are decorated, ask a grownup to poke a hole in one side and out the other of each section.

- Your child can count things in groups of ten, matching the items to the sections of the snake.

- Help your child draw and write silly stories about the snake.

- Make a family of snakes, each with a different number of sections.

Put It Together

Now, you're ready to put the sections together:

1) Tie a knot at one end of the string and lace on a section, just as you would lace on beads.

2) Tie another knot to keep the section in place.

3) Lace on all the sections in the same way. If you leave a little extra string between the sections, your snake can wiggle like a real snake!

Count It Out!

Trace the numbers as you count the fingers. Then answer the question.

1 2 3 4 5 6 7 8 9

How many fingers show how old you are? _____

Color in the right number of fingers.

Domino Play

Did you know that most games use numbers? It's true! Numbers help you play outside games like Hopscotch and inside games that use spinners and cards. Numbers also help you keep score.

One game that uses numbers is dominoes. Take out your dominoes, or use the next page to make some.

🕐 Play the Game

You can play dominoes many ways. Here's a game that's good for two or three players:

1) Divide the dominoes so that each player has the same number. Put the extra tiles to the side.

2) The first player puts a domino on the table.

3) The next player tries to add a domino by counting and matching spots.

4) Players take turns trying to add to the domino chain. If a player can't make a match, he or she must wait another turn.

5) The player who runs out of dominoes first wins.

Play a 5 here.

Or, play a 4 here.

💡 You can use dominoes to help introduce basic math facts. For example, a domino with 3 spots on one side and 2 spots on the other illustrates this number sentence: 3 + 2 = 5.

✋ On the following pencil page, your child can practice counting and writing numbers. If you wish to use the page to make dominoes, make a copy of it before your child counts and colors the spots.

Domino Cards

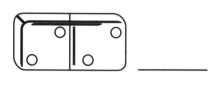

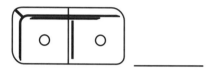 _____

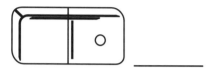 _____

Color and count the domino spots. Then write the number the domino shows.

 _____

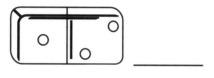 _____

 _____

 _____

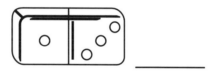 _____

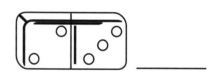 _____

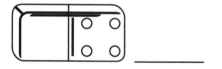 _____

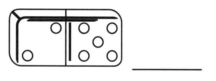 _____

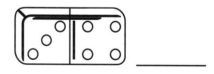 _____

 _____

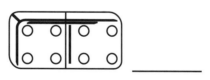 _____

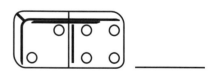 _____

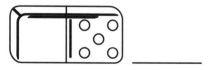 _____

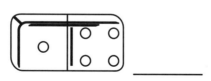 _____

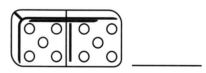 _____

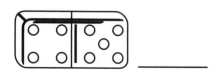 _____

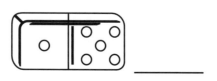 _____

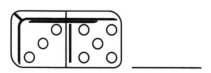 _____

A Counting Rhyme

Do you know the counting rhyme "One, Two, Buckle My Shoe"? How about the rhyme where the ants go marching in? There are many counting rhymes that you can sing or jump rope to. You can even turn them into finger plays.

Make a Finger Play

Here's the first verse to a counting rhyme you may know:

Five little monkeys jumping on the bed.
One fell off and bumped his head.
Mama called the doctor and the doctor said,
"No more monkeys jumping on the bed!"

Did you hear any words that rhyme with **bed**?
What number would start the next verse? Yes, **four**!

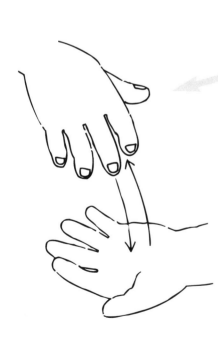

Turn this rhyme into a finger play.

• Hold up five fingers to begin.

• Then make up hand actions to go with the words.

How many fingers will you hold up to start the next verse?

Say the rhyme until there are no more monkeys left on the bed. How will you end your finger play?

Turn your child's favorite counting rhyme into a book. Write each line on a separate sheet of paper. Then ask your child to illustrate each frame.

On the pencil page that follows, your child can choose rhymes from the pictures at the top of the page or create his or her own rhymes. For example: "When I was two, I had a blue shoe."

Rhyme a Number

1

2

Can you make up rhymes for these numbers? See if these pictures help you with your rhymes.

3

4

Picture Names: *shoe, sun, tree, door*

Make a Counting Book

Think about the counting books you've seen. What did they count? Animals? Shapes? Something else?

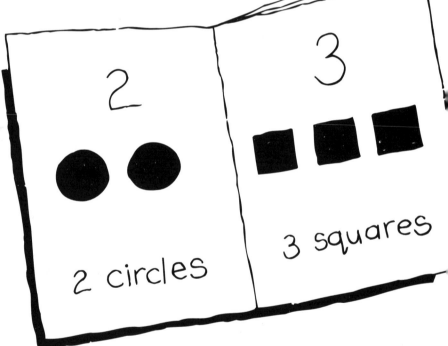 Make a Counting Book

You can make a counting book of your own. Here's how:

1) Think about what you want your counting book to show. This counting book is about shapes.

2) Take out ten pieces of paper. Write a number from **1** to **10** at the top of each page.

3) Draw a picture to go with each number. Remember, your picture should show how *many*.

4) When you're done, you can make a cover for your counting book. Then, ask a grownup to help you staple or tie the pages together.

On the following page, your child can practice listening for beginning sounds. After your child completes the page, he or she might suggest other words that begin with the same sounds as *two* and *ten*, *four* and *five*, and *six* and *seven*.

Beginning Sounds

Match the numbers with the same beginning sound. Color the numbers. Use a different color for each match.

Kitchen Art

Did you know you can use uncooked pasta to make beautiful works of art? Try one or more of these ideas.

Noodle Necklaces

Measure and cut a piece of yarn that is the right length for a necklace. Then, string pasta wheels and elbow macaroni onto the yarn to make a necklace. Count and change shapes to make different patterns.

Pasta Pencil Holder

Cover an empty juice container with brightly colored paper. Paste different pasta shapes to the outside to make a pencil holder.

Macaroni Mosaics

Draw a picture on cardboard and paste uncooked macaroni onto the drawing. Paint the pasta to look like colored tiles.

Same or Different

Play "Same or Different" as you make your kitchen art. One player says two words. The other player says whether or not the two words begin with the same sound. Try these words!

- milk, macaroni (same)
- pasta, noodle (different)

 The pencil page that follows is one of many beginning sound pages. To help your child focus on beginning sounds, say each picture name slowly, emphasizing the initial consonant.

M is for Monkey

------- Mm

Trace **Mm**. Color the pictures that begin with **m**. Then draw a line to help the monkey follow the **m** words and get through the maze.

The End

Picture Names: *monkey, jet, hat, lion, milk, mop, meat, cup, banana, mitten*

Beginning Sound
Dictionary

Ss

6 **six**

7 **seven**

seal   **sock**

You know that **6** and **7** are different numbers. Count to **7** to see how they are different. Now say the words **six** and **seven**. How are they alike? Yes, they begin with the same sound and the same letter, **s**. Name some other words that begin like **six** and **seven**.

Listen for <u>s</u>

You can use what you know about sounds and letters to start a Beginning Sound Dictionary. Look in magazines and catalogs for pictures of things whose names begin with the sound for **s**. Cut out the pictures.

Organize the pages in a three-ring binder. As the dictionary grows, use tabbed dividers to identify and separate letters. Get a head start on new pages by having your child cut out and save pictures of interest. Store the pictures until your child is ready to use them.

Make a Dictionary Page

Here's how to make a dictionary page:

1) Write **Ss** at the top of a piece of paper.

2) Glue the pictures that begin with the sound for **s** on the page.

3) Label the pictures, or ask someone to help you write the names.

As you learn more about sounds and letters, add new pages to your dictionary.

S is for Seven

_____
_ S s _

Color the pictures that begin with **s**. Then practice writing **Ss** next to those pictures.

Picture Names: *sock, six, four, sun, soap, balloon*

Books to Share

Counting books are so numerous that many libraries and bookstores set aside special shelves to accommodate them. Here are a few titles you and your child may enjoy.

The M&M's® Brand Chocolate Candies Counting Book by Barbara Barbieri McGrath (Charlesbridge, 1994). Grab a bag of these candies and follow the directions to sort, count, and eat your way through the book.

One White Sail by S. T. Garne (Green Tiger, 1992). The rhyming text and vivid watercolors help convey the sights and sounds of a Caribbean island.

Anno's Counting Book by Mitsumasa Anno (Harper, 1977). This wordless counting book begins with one house on a snowy hillside and shows the growth of a town through the twelve months of the year.

Roll Over! A Counting Song by Merle Peek (Clarion, 1981). Ten sleepy animals fall out of a little boy's bed in this picture book version of a favorite counting song. Save this one for reading and singing at bedtime.

More books you might enjoy:

How Many How Many How Many by Rick Walton (Candlewick, 1993). Readers count from one to twelve to answer questions about nursery rhymes, seasons, insects, and more.

Five Little Monkeys Jumping on the Bed by Eileen Christelow (Clarion, 1989). Five little monkeys fall off the bed one by one.

Teddy Bears 1 to 10 by Susanna Gretz (Four Winds, 1986). Ten teddy bears are washed, dried, dyed, and returned home in time for tea.

This Old Man by Carol Jones (Houghton, 1990). A traditional rhyme is updated as a grandfather and a little girl spend a day together.

 Suggestions

Preview the title and pictures with your child on the next page. Then read the rhyme together.

✱ Help your child to use picture clues and what he or she already knows about numbers to decode the number words.

✱ On a second reading, your child can listen for rhyming words and suggest additional words that rhyme.

After completing the story, encourage your child to color it in and share it with other family members.

My Counting Rhyme

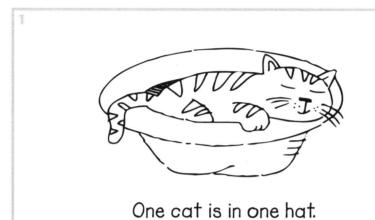

One cat is in one hat.

Two pigs are in two wigs.

Three frogs are on three logs.

* My Story

4

Four bugs are on four mugs.

5

Five _____ are on five _____ .

Animal Fair

CHAPTER 3

The Animal Fair

I went to the animal fair;

The birds and the beasts were there.

The old baboon by the light of the moon

Was combing his auburn hair.

The funniest was the monk;

He sat on the elephant's trunk.

The elephant sneezed and fell on his knees,

But what became of the monk?

A Note About Animal Fair

Most children are intrigued by animals. We keep animals as pets; we train them to work for us. We also flock to animal parks to see those we might otherwise never meet. The activities in *Animal Fair* explore the fascinating world of animals while providing practice with these reading skills:

PHONICS/INITIAL CONSONANTS: Four more initial letter-sound correspondences—*d, h, b,* and *g*—are introduced in *Animal Fair.*

PHONICS/PHONOGRAMS: Once children have grasped the concept of rhyme and have learned several letter-sound correspondences, they are ready for phonograms, or word families. One common phonogram is *-at,* which can be used to make such words as *bat, cat, hat, mat, pat,* and so on. Your child can practice *-at* and *-ug* in this chapter.

FANTASY/REALISM: The stories kindergarteners are reading in school may be realistic or fanciful. Your child is learning to distinguish between realism and fantasy by thinking about story characters and deciding whether or not they could exist in real life. Point out that our panda mascot is a make-believe animal character. As you read stories or watch television programs together, talk about which characters are real and which are make-believe.

CATEGORIZE/CLASSIFY: We use this important "thinking" skill every day, yet most of us probably don't remember when or how we first learned it. Invite your child to help you do sorting tasks around the house. Talk about why you group certain things together, and ask your child to suggest other ways to group things.

At this age, children are also learning important reading strategies, such as making predictions and monitoring (mentioned in Chapters 1 and 2). Another strategy is *evaluating,* which involves making judgments about a story. During and after reading with your child, you might ask questions such as the following:

- Did you like the story? Why or why not?
- Did the book answer your questions?
- Did you learn anything new? What was it?

Animal Safari

Safari Walk

What animals live in your neighborhood? Go on a safari walk to find out! You can look for animals everywhere–on the ground, up a tree, in the air, and in the water.

What animals did you see? A cat or a dog? A bird or a squirrel? On a fresh sheet of paper, draw a picture to show these animals.

Picture Safari

Go on another animal safari. This time, let your fingers walk through old magazines. Cut out pictures of the animals you find.

How could you sort these pictures? You might arrange them into these groups:

Save the pictures for other activities.

| Animals with fur and animals with feathers | → | Animals that are big and animals that are small |

Not a good day for a safari walk?

Go on a "TV safari." Watch a nature program and talk about what you and your child learned.

Sorting is an important skill. Provide opportunities for your child to practice sorting by helping to sort laundry, match socks, put away silverware, and group toys.

Many children's books feature make-believe animals. As you share stories with your child, talk about how fantasy animals are different from real animals.

Animal Posters

Remember the animal pictures from "Picture Safari"? You'll need them for this activity, too. If you haven't collected any pictures yet, you can start now. Look through old magazines or catalogs to find pictures of all kinds of animals, and cut them out.

◑ Making the Posters

Sort your animal pictures into four groups:

1) Animals as Pets
2) Animals in the Woods
3) Animals on a Farm
4) Animals in a Zoo

Pets

cat

dog

fish

bird

Pick one group. How about pets? Write the group name "Pets" at the top of a large sheet of paper. Then, glue the pet pictures onto the paper and label each one.

📝 Your child can use the pencil page that follows as a workmat for sorting the animal pictures into groups. As your child sorts, point out that some animals can belong to more than one group.

✋ Labeling pictures will help your child make the connection between printed and spoken words. As you label, say the picture name slowly and ask your child to provide the beginning letter.

Sort It Out!

Think of an animal for each group. Draw the animal and label it.

An Animal as a Pet

An Animal on a Farm

An Animal in the Zoo

An Animal in the Woods

My Very Own Pet Rock

Have you ever thought about all the different kinds of pets people have? Do you know someone who has a cat? A fish? How about a guinea pig? Make a list of pets. Which is your favorite?

Making a Pet Rock

Turn a rock into a pet! First, find a rock with a shape you like. Look for one about the size of your fist. Good places to find rocks are in your backyard, an empty lot, or a field. Here are some ways to turn your rock into a pet:

- Think about what the head and face will look like. Plan how to show the face on the rock.

- Paint or draw eyes, ears, a nose, and a mouth on the rock. You can also use buttons, dried beans, yarn, or pieces of cloth.

- Make a home for your pet rock! Use an old shoe box. Write your pet's name on the box.

- What will make your pet happy? Talk about your ideas.

With your child, hunt for a rock on your next outing and store it for a rainy day. Or, instead of a rock, your child can make a pet potato.

Talk about the kind of care your child's pet rock would need if it were real. Ask your child to help you draw up a schedule for feeding, walking, and so on.

D is for Dog

Dd

Color the pictures that begin with d. Then practice writing Dd next to those pictures.

_____

_____

_____

_____

_____

_____

Picture Names: *cat, door, doll, lamp, desk, dinosaur*

47

Put Me in the Zoo

Where would you go to see lions, tigers, monkeys, and bears? That's right, a zoo! What other animals might you see at a zoo?

🕐 A New Animal for the Zoo

Now use what you know about real zoo animals to create a make-believe animal for the zoo. It might be two or more real animals put together.

You decide!

- How will the animal look?
- How will the animal act?
- What will the animal eat?

Draw a picture of your animal, and give it a name.

Your child can also make a model of his or her imaginary animal, using yarn, clay, fabric, boxes, buttons, and other materials.

Extend the activity by asking your child to tell a story about the animal, draw pictures to show where it lives and what it eats, or tell how it is like real animals and how it is different.

H is for Hippo

Trace Hh. Color the pictures that begin with h. Then draw a line to help the hippo follow the h words.

The End

Picture Names: *hippo, mop, hand, door, jeans, hook, horse, bell, buttons, hose*

Kitchen Critters

You can use food to make your own animal critters, and they can be tasty treats, too! Here are three ideas to start you off. (Be sure to ask a grownup to help you.)

Caterpillar Bananas

Peel a banana. Use pretzel sticks to make the caterpillar's legs and its antennae.

Ants on a Log

Cut celery stalks into 3-inch "logs." Spread cream cheese onto the celery stalks. Stick raisin "ants" on the cream cheese. Enjoy!

Salad Mouse

Put half a pear, flat side down, on a piece of lettuce. Add a raisin "nose" and raisin "eyes" to the pointy end of the pear. Use slivers of carrot for the mouse's "whiskers."

Play "Real or Make-Believe" as you eat your critter. One player says a sentence about an animal. The other says whether it's "real" or "make-believe." Try these sentences:

A pig can fly.   (make-believe)
A duck quacks.   (real)

Let your child do as much "work" as possible when making the critter snacks. A vegetable parer comes in handy for making carrot-sliver whiskers.

50

B is for Bug

Bb

Trace the letters Bb. Who's hiding? Color each space with a picture name that begins with b. What did you find?

Picture Names: *hat, milk, fox, bus, ball, bug, bat, bed, sun, goat*

Make a Songbook

What sound does a cow make? If you said "Moo," you're ready to sing "Old MacDonald Had a Farm."

Goat

Maa.Maa

A Songbook of Your Own

You can make an "Old MacDonald" songbook to read or to help others sing with you. Here's how:

- Gather together paper and crayons. Make a drawing for each farm animal you want in your book.

- On the drawing, write the name of the animal and the sound it makes. Try to write the first letter of each word yourself. A grownup can help you write the rest of the word.

- Staple or tie the pages together to make a book!

Does your child have a favorite animal song? Turn this song into a book. Write the words, line for line, on different sheets of paper. Then ask your child to draw the pictures. Read, or sing, the book together.

G is for Goat

_____
G g

Color the pictures that begin with **g**. Then practice writing **Gg** next to those pictures.

Picture Names: _girl, game, pear, goat, desk, gate_

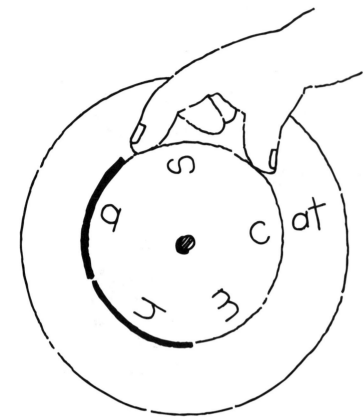

Word Wheels

Here's a riddle for you. How do you change a **cat** into a **hat**? Give up? Change the first letter!

🕐 Spin a New Word

What else can you change a **cat** into? Make a word wheel to find out. Here's how:

1) Take two paper plates. Cut the round border off one, so you have one smaller circle.

2) Print **at** by the edge of the big circle.

3) Print the letters **b, c, h, m,** and **s** around the edge of the small circle.

4) Use a paper fastener to attach the small circle to the big circle in the center so that the small circle turns.

5) Turn the small circle to read the words!

Now make a word wheel to see what you can change a **bug** into. Use the letters **b, d, h,** and **m** with **ug**.

This activity uses letter-sound associations already introduced in the book. If you wish, add *f, p,* and *r* to the *-at* wheel or add *j* and *r* to the *-ug* wheel. If your child has trouble reading a word, help him or her isolate the beginning sound and the ending. Then show how to blend the sounds together. For the word *bat* you might say: "This word begins like *bear* and ends like *cat.*"

The pencil page that follows provides practice in reading words from the *-at* and *-ug* word families.

Can you read these words? Draw lines to match the words to the pictures.

Picture-Word Matchup

bat

mat

cat

hat

bug

rug

jug

mug

Picture Names: *hat, bat, cat, mat; jug, bug, mug, rug*

Look at all the things I can do!

☐ I can say and write the letters of the alphabet.

☐ I can name colors.

☐ I can say and write numbers.

☐ I can rhyme words.

☐ I can name words that begin with the letters **b, d, g, h, m,** and **s.**

☐ I can name the letter that stands for the sound at the beginning of words like **monkey, seal, bear, dog, horse,** and **goat.**

☐ I can read words that end with **at** and **ug.**

☐ I can look for details in pictures, words, and the other things I see.

☐ I can sort things by thinking about their size, shape, color, or how they are used.

☐ I can tell if stories are real or make-believe.

Books to Share

Here are some titles you might want to share with your child. As you read the books, note which animals are real and which are make-believe.

Bears in the Forest
by Karen Wallace (Candlewick, 1994). Learn facts about real bears as you follow a mother bear and her cubs.

Feathers for Lunch
by Lois Ehlert (Harcourt, 1989). A variety of birds is introduced as a house cat tries to catch one bird for lunch. See how many of the birds you can find in your own neighborhood.

Happy Birthday, Duck
by Eve Bunting (Clarion, 1988). The birthday gifts Duck receives don't make sense until Tortoise arrives with the last gift. Before you read the ending, ask your child to predict what the gift will be.

Dog In, Cat Out
by Gillian Rubinstein (Ticknor, 1993). Using only the words in the title, this book tells the comings and goings of two families' pets. Invite your child to read this book to you.

More books you might enjoy:

Ask Mr. Bear by Majorie Flack (Macmillan, 1932). A child asks all the animals on the farm for birthday gift ideas for his mother.

Biggest, Strongest, Fastest by Steve Jenkins (Houghton, 1995). Learn about fourteen real animals and the records they hold.

Sheep in a Jeep by Nancy Shaw (Houghton, 1986). Some simple-minded sheep take a ride in this rhyming adventure.

Sleepy Bear by Lydia Dabcovich (Dutton, 1982). A bear gets ready to hibernate, sleeps through the winter, and wakes up again in spring.

 Suggestions

Read the title on the next page and look at the pictures with your child. Ask what this story is about. Then read together.

✱ Help your child use picture clues and what he or she already knows about animals to figure out the words.

✱ Point out the language pattern: The (animal) said, "(sound)." Your child can draw a picture and complete the sentence to finish the story.

What Did It Say?

The cat said, "Meow!"

The dog said, "Bow-wow!"

The duck said, "Quack!"

The cow said, "Moo!"

The _____ said, "_____!"

Friends and Family

CHAPTER 4

The Very Nicest Place

The fish lives in the brook.

The bird lives in the tree.

But home's the very nicest place

For a little child like me.

A Note About Friends and Family

Whether kindergarten is a child's first experience in a classroom or the next step up from child care and preschool, he or she is sure to find the first foray into school to be quite an adventure—both academically and socially. Suddenly, a child's world extends beyond the family to include new people and new friends. *Friends and Family* explores old and new relationships, while offering plenty of practice on these reading skills:

PHONICS/INITIAL CONSONANTS: Four more initial letter-sound correspondences—*f, p, c,* and *k*—are introduced.

PHONICS/PHONOGRAMS: Two more phonograms, or word families— *-ig* as in *pig* and *-it* as in *sit*—are introduced.

DRAWING CONCLUSIONS: One way authors engage readers is to let them figure out some things on their own. Many kindergartners are learning to use story information along with what they already know to draw conclusions about characters and events.

CAUSE/EFFECT: Children learn that in stories, just as in real life, one event often causes another event to happen. You can help your child identify cause-effect relationships by asking *Why-Because* questions: *Why* did Amanda take an umbrella to school? (*because* it looked like rain.) *Why* did Amanda get wet walking home from school? (*because* she forgot her umbrella at school, *because* she got caught in the rain.)

One important reading strategy kindergartners are learning to use is integrated word analysis, or, more simply, they are learning to *think about words*. Here, children learn several approaches they can take to figure out a word that they may not recognize while you read together. These approaches include:

- thinking about the beginning sound to decode the word;
- looking for familiar word parts (word families) to decode the word;
- thinking about a word that makes sense in the sentence to read the word or learn its meaning;
- looking at illustrations for clues for reading (or pronouncing) the word or getting its meaning.

My Family Is Special

Some families are big. Some are small. Each family is different and special in its own way. You can show what's special about your family by making a family flag.

A Family Flag

Think about what makes your family special to you. Write down your ideas. These questions might help you:

- What do we like to eat? Where do we like to go?

- Do we have special ways to celebrate birthdays or holidays?

- Do we have special pets?

When you're ready to begin, here are some ideas for making your flag:

Draw or cut out pictures of the things you want on the flag.

Paste the pictures onto a large sheet of paper.

Decorate the flag with colored paper, ribbon, or stickers.

Add your family's name to the flag before hanging it.

Family flags, like coats of arms, came into use during the Middle Ages to identify individuals and groups on the battlefield. If you'd like to include some of these symbols on your flag, look for books on heraldry in your library.

A flag can show something about a family's heritage, hobbies, or the likes and dislikes of individual family members. You might also try one of these ideas:
- Make your flag out of felt or fabric.
- Use family photos to illustrate the flag.
- Make a flag for each family member.

Friends and Family Tree

A family tree shows all the people in your family. A "Friends and Family Tree" goes one step further. It shows the people in your family **and** your friends!

◐ Make the Tree

To make a "Friends and Family Tree," you'll need construction paper and a place to put the tree, like an empty wall or a refrigerator door. Draw and cut out the tree trunk and some branches. Tape them onto your space.

Make the Leaves

Once your tree is ready, cut out a leaf for each friend and family member you'd like on your tree. You can trace the leaf patterns on page 63.

Write a name on each leaf. Say each name and listen to the beginning sound. What letter does the name start with?

Put Them All Together

Read each name as you tape the leaves on the tree. Does the name belong to a friend or to a family member?

Say each name slowly to help your child determine the first letter. Spell the rest of the name to provide writing practice.

Use the following pencil page as a pattern for making the leaves. Or, copy the page and cut out the leaves.

Friends and Family Leaves

Here are some leaves you can use for your "Friends and Family Tree." Trace the leaves so you can make as many as you need.

63

A Book of Friends

How would you like to visit your friends every day? You can, if you make a special friendship book!

Jamie and I ride bikes together.

◑ Design Friendship Pages

Begin your book by making a friendship page for each friend. Draw pictures on the page to show what you like about this friend or to show something you like to do with this friend.

Assemble the Book

Once your pages are ready, put together your friendship book. Here are some ideas you might use:

- Write the friend's name on the page.

- Write a sentence to describe your friend.

- Make a cover for the book.

- Staple the finished pages together to create a book. Or, tie the pages together with ribbon or colored yarn.

This activity can span several days, with your child making one or two pages a sitting. Share experiences your child has had with each person. Ask questions to focus on cause-and-effect relationships: Why did Jamie fall off his bike? Why didn't he see the hole? Why was he looking at you? and so on.

F is for Family

_____ _
- - - - -

Color the pictures that begin with f. Then practice writing Ff next to those pictures.

Picture Names: _feather, fish, five, hose, duck, fox_

65

A Family Breakfast

What shape is a pancake? If you said circle, you're right. But have you ever thought about making pancake **squares**? They taste just as good as circle pancakes.

What You'll Need

- 2 cups of pancake mix (and the ingredients listed on the box for a 2-cup mix)

- 1/2 cup raisins or blueberries (optional)

- 15 x 10 inch baking pan or a deep cookie sheet

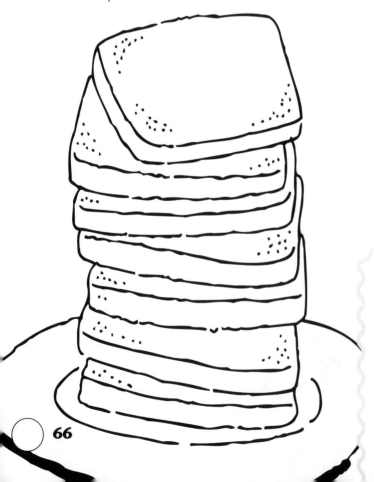

What to Do

Here's how to make pancake squares:

1) Ask a grownup to turn the oven to 425°.

2) While the oven warms, make the batter. Remember to follow the directions for 2 cups of mix.

3) If you want, add raisins.

4) Pour the batter into a greased pan.

5) Bake for 10 minutes or until the edges are light brown and the top springs back when touched.

6) Have the grownup take the pan out of the oven and cut the pancakes into 2-inch squares.

Serve the squares with butter, syrup, or powdered sugar. Mmm, good!

Boxed mixes combine words and pictures in their directions. Encourage your child to read the directions with you. Your child can also help set the table, gather ingredients, and mix the batter.

After your child completes the *p* pencil page, ask if the pig might like pancake squares! Encourage your child to explain his or her conclusion.

P is for Pig

P
p

Trace **Pp**. Color the pictures that begin with **p**. Then draw a line to help the pig follow the **p** words to the end of the maze.

The End

Picture Names: *pig, banana, jar, bed, pan, pillow, sink, pencil, pancakes, milk*

Paper Presents

If you could give each person in your family a present, what would it be? Like most kids, you probably can't buy much. But paper presents can be great, no-money gifts. Read on to find out how to make them!

Pick a Present

Look through old catalogs to find presents that people in your family might like. Cut out your favorites. Then use the pictures to make paper presents for your family.

- Paste each gift onto a piece of paper.

- Write a message on the paper, if you wish.

- Decorate the page with other drawings.

- Roll up the paper, and tie it with yarn or ribbon.

- Give each person his or her paper present.

For Nana

While looking through the catalogs, invite your child to use word and picture clues to read the item names. Also talk about what you know about each person to draw conclusions that will help your child choose an appropriate gift.

C is for Card

Cc

Color the pictures that begin with c. Then practice writing Cc next to those pictures.

Picture Names: *car, cat, candle, boots, rabbit, camel*

Fly a Friendship Kite

Here's a nifty way to take your friends and family kite flying, even if you—or they—can't go in person.

◑ Make a Friendship Kite

Ask a grownup to help you follow the directions to put together a store-bought kite. Or, try making your own friendship kite. Here's how:

- Cut out a kite shape from a large piece of paper. Decorate it with pictures, glitter, or glow-in-the-dark stickers.

- Tie a string to the kite and hang it on your bedroom wall.

◑ Make Friendship Cards

- Make name cards for each person you want to go kite flying with you. Here's what to do:

1) Cut out a square for each person.

2) Write a name on each paper square.

3) Punch a hole in the middle of the square.

4) Slide the card up the string through the hole.

- Read the names as you hang the cards on the string.

If your child likes making kites, you can find many books on kites in the local library.

If you want to fly a real kite, use notebook paper for the names (so that the cards won't weigh down the string). Cut a slit from one corner to the center hole so that the cards will slide up the string.

K is for Kite

K_ _ _ _ _ _ _

What flies high in the sky? Color each space with a picture that begins with **k**. What did you find?

Picture Names: *plane, milk, mouse, kitchen, key, six, hat, king, kangaroo, boots, lamp*

Games to Play

Do you like to play games with friends and family members? If so, here are two games to try:

Build a Word

To play "Build a Word," you create new words from given words. First, make letter cards for **b, d, f, h, p,** and **s.** Then use the game board on page 73. Here's how:

- Put all the letter cards face down on the table.

- Place your markers on START.

- Take turns choosing a card. Place it by the first space, and read the word. If it's a real word, move your marker forward one space. The first player to get HOME wins.

Construct game boards like the one on the following pencil page to practice phonograms like -at and -ug.

As your child gains proficiency with "Build a Word," add more letter cards. For "Build a Story," help your child transcribe one of the stories and illustrate it as a book.

Build a Story

Write the words you created in "Build a Word" on separate cards. Then play "Build a Story." Here's how:

- Start a story about a pig. You might say, "Pig wanted to go to school and learn to read like real children."

- Pick a card and use the word to tell the next part of the story. For **wig,** you might say, "One morning, Pig put on a **wig** and got on the school bus."

- Take turns picking words and using them to add to the story.

Race Home

How many new words can you read? Use your letter cards to find out. Play the game with a friend or family member. Who can reach HOME first?

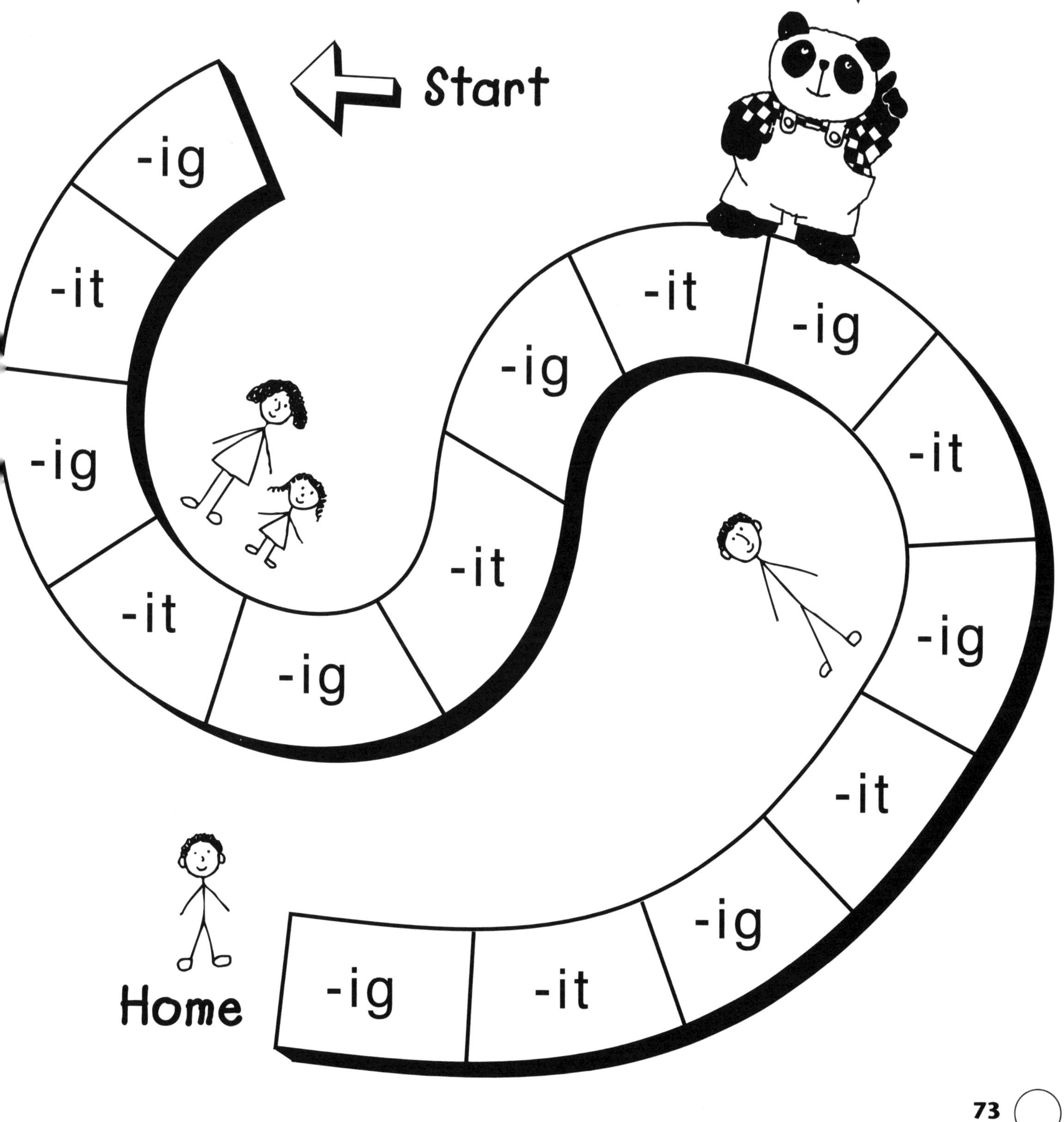

Start

-ig

-it

-ig

-it

-ig

-it

-ig

-it

-ig

-it

-ig

-it

-ig

-it

-ig

-it

-ig

Home

-ig

-it

Books to Share

Books on families and friends are as many and as varied as kinds of families and friends. Here are a few titles to choose from.

Jamaica's Find by Juanita Havill (Houghton, 1986). Jamaica battles her conscience until she returns a stuffed animal she found to the Lost-and-Found. Good for drawing conclusions and cause-and-effect relationships.

Guess How Much I Love You by Sam McBratney (Candlewick, 1994). During a bedtime game, little Nutbrown Hare demonstrates his love for his father, who in turn shows that the love is returned even more.

Just Like Daddy by Frank Asch (Aladdin, 1989). A little bear cub does everything "just like Daddy," until he catches a big fish "just like Mommy."

Peter's Chair by Ezra Jack Keats (Harper, 1967). Peter's old highchair and crib have been painted pink for the baby. Feeling left out, Peter decides to run away and take his little chair with him.

More books you might enjoy:

Big Sister and Little Sister by Charlotte Zolotow (Harper, 1990). Siblings will enjoy this story about a big sister and little sister who learn to care for and comfort each other.

Frog and Toad Are Friends by Arnold Lobel (Harper, 1970). Frog and Toad's special friendship is explored in five short stories that will leave children asking for more.

I Go with My Family to Grandma's by Riki Levinson (Puffin, 1992). A girl tells how her family and her cousins' families travel to get to Grandma's.

Do You Want to Be My Friend? by Eric Carle (Crowell, 1971). In this nearly wordless picture book, a little mouse follows animal tails from page to page, looking for a friend.

Suggestions

With your child, read the title and look at the pictures on the next page. Help your child draw conclusions about the pictures by asking: Which picture shows Panda's family? Which shows Panda's friends? How do you know? Then read the story together.

✱ Invite your child to write about his or her family and friends, using the last two story frames. Then invite your child to illustrate the story.

* My Story

My Friends and Family

Here is my family.
We like to climb trees.

Here are my friends.
We like to play games.

3

Here is my family.
We like to _____ .

4

Here are my friends.
We like to _____ .

CHAPTER 5

The Way I Feel

If You're Happy and You Know It

If you're happy and you know it, clap your hands.

If you're happy and you know it, clap your hands.

If you're happy and you know it,

Then your face will surely show it.

If you're happy and you know it, clap your hands.

A Note About The Way I Feel

Kindergarten is a time of discovery. Children begin to take a closer look at the world around them and the ways in which it affects them. In this chapter, children will explore the way they feel, from their basic five senses to their emotions. They'll also practice these reading skills:

PHONICS/INITIAL CONSONANTS: In this chapter, the initial letter-sound correspondences *w*, *l*, *t*, and *n* are introduced.

PHONICS/PHONOGRAMS: Two more phonograms, or word families— *-ot* as in *hot* and *-and* as in *hand*—are introduced.

STORY STRUCTURE: As children are exposed to more and more books, they begin to learn that stories have many common parts. You can help your child recognize common parts, such as setting, characters, and plot, by asking questions like these:

- Where does the story take place?
- Who is in the story?
- What happens in the story?

TOPIC/MAIN IDEA: Most kindergartners first learn about topic and main ideas through nonfiction books. They learn that stories that give information usually convey one or more important, or main, ideas about a topic. You can help your child identify the topic and main ideas by asking questions such as:

- What is the whole story about?
- What idea(s) does the author want to share about (the topic)?

In the preceding chapters, we've identified strategies that help readers to better understand and enjoy what they read. One strategy that helps to check children's understanding is *summarizing.* Here, young readers use what they know about story structure and topic and main ideas to tell, in their own words, what a selection is all about. To practice summarizing with your child, ask questions that will help your child identify the setting, characters, plot, and/or topic and main ideas of a selection.

♪ Sing a Song ♪♪

What do you do when you feel happy? How about when you feel sad? You can tell about some of the ways you feel and the things you do by singing a song.

Think Happy Thoughts

The poem "If You're Happy and You Know It" is also a song. Try singing it.

What else do you do when you're happy? Do you laugh? Dance? List your ideas. Use them to sing about being happy!

More Feelings

Here are more feelings you can sing about. What actions can you use to show each feeling?

- If you're sad and you know it,

  _____ .

- If you're hungry and you know it,

  _____ .

- If you're proud and you know it,

  _____ .

- If you're angry and you know it,

  _____ .

- If you're excited and you know it,

  _____ .

- If you're scared and you know it,

  _____ .

Help your child stick to the main idea by talking about the appropriateness of specific actions for different feelings. You can also build awareness of feelings by discussing them as they come up.

Play a guessing game. Take turns suggesting and pantomiming different actions while someone else names the emotion.

What's in a Face?

What do you think when you see a smile? A frown? Tears? Faces tell a lot about the way people feel. Take a closer look!

🕐 Feelings in Faces

Look through magazines to find pictures of people. Try to decide how each person feels. Use these questions to help you decide:

How do I feel when I look this way?

What does this person's face look like?

Is there anything else in the picture that helps me decide how the person feels?

🕐 Here Come the Clowns

Clowns use make-up to create happy and sad faces. You can use markers and paper plates. Draw a happy clown face on one plate and a sad face on the other.

Think about the things that make you happy or sad. Use what you know to tell stories that explain why one clown is happy and the other is sad.

Use the clown faces to share the day's events with your child. Take turns relating events and holding up the appropriate clown face.

As you read together, help your child use his or her own experiences along with the words and pictures to decide how a character feels. This helps your child to better understand a story and evaluate a character's actions.

Happy or Sad?

Think about things that make you happy or sad. Draw pictures to show your ideas.

 happy

 sad

A Week of Feelings

How can you be happy one day and sad the next? Feelings change all the time. How often do they change in a week? Let's find out.

Monday

The big storm made me feel scared.

Make a "Feelings" Page

Take out seven pieces of paper. Ask a grownup to help you label each page with a day of the week—**Monday, Tuesday,** and so on.

Sit down each night to talk about your day and how you felt. Draw a picture to show your feelings. You can label the picture with a feeling word or a sentence that describes your feelings.

Make a Book

At the end of the week, put the pages in order and staple them to make a book. Here are more ideas you might try:

- Label other people or places in your pictures.

- Tell a story about each picture to explain why something made you feel a certain way.

- Make a cover for the book.

Help your child use words and pictures to keep a kindergarten journal of his or her experiences and feelings. Revisit the journal often.

Since journals help build reading and writing skills, many teachers encourage children to keep classroom journals.

W is for Week

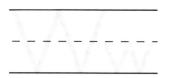

Color the pictures that begin with **w**. Then practice writing **Ww** next to those pictures.

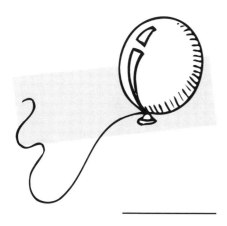

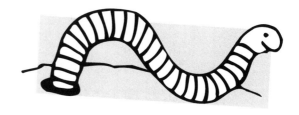

Picture Names: *water, candle, balloon, wagon, wood, worm*

My Five Senses

What sounds make you happy? The bell on an ice-cream truck? The purr of a kitten? Something else?

Can you name a sound that makes you sad? Read on to find out more about the things we hear, see, smell, taste, and touch.

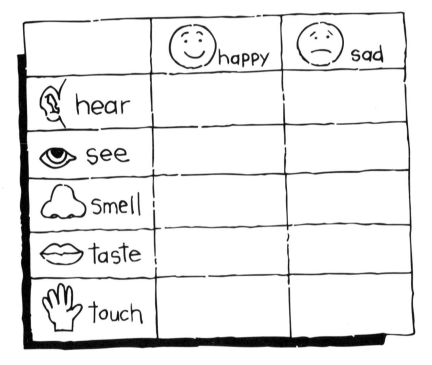

	😊 happy	😞 sad
👂 hear		
👁 see		
👃 smell		
👄 taste		
✋ touch		

 ## The Five Senses

You have five senses that help you learn about the world and make you feel different ways. Here's what they are:

- Hearing: We hear with our ears.

- Seeing: We see with our eyes.

- Smelling: We smell with our noses.

- Tasting: We taste with our mouths.

- Touching: We touch with our hands.

Think about things you hear, see, smell, taste, and touch that make you feel happy or sad. Draw your ideas on the chart. Or, make a bigger chart if you have a lot of ideas. How would other people in your family fill in the chart?

With your child, talk about other feelings and how the five senses might contribute to each one. You might ask: What sounds make you feel scared? Excited? Lonely?

Use the items on the next pencil page to help your child see that we often use multiple senses to experience things. For example: We can see, touch, smell, and taste a lemon.

L is for Lion

Trace Ll. Color the pictures that begin with l. Then draw a line to help the lion follow the l words to the end of the maze.

The End

Picture Names: *lion, lamp, doll, lock, corn, lemon, monkey, bed, saw, leaf*

Taste Test

 Most people have foods they like and foods they don't like. Think about the foods you don't like. Why don't you like them? Is it the way they look? How they smell? The way they taste?

As you and your child classify foods by taste, think of other words that help describe the foods, such as *crunchy, smooth, juicy, wet, dry, hot,* and *cold.*

The human tongue perceives four tastes—sweet, salty, sour, and bitter. It also has receptors for heat, cold, pain, and texture. But to distinguish flavors, like vanilla, the tongue must work with the receptors of the nose.

Do a Taste Test

Ask a grownup to help you find different things to taste. Put a tiny bit of one on your tongue. Think about these questions:

- Is it **sweet** like sugar?
- Is it **sour** like a lemon?
- Is it **salty** like salt?
- Is it **bitter** like coffee?

Tasting with Your Nose

Your tongue tells you if something is sweet, sour, salty, or bitter. But your nose tells you what flavor it is. Try this:

1) Get out two flavors of ice cream.

2) Close your eyes and take a taste of ice cream. Can you name the flavor?

3) Do the same thing, but this time close your eyes and hold your nose. Now can you name the flavor?

T is for Taste

Color the spaces with pictures that begin with t. What did you find?

Picture Names: *table, tent, ball, four, top, bike, kitchen, deer, tiger, camel*

Busy Hands

All day long, your hands are busy. They draw and write. They work and play. They feed you, wash you, and dress you. Most important, your hands help you learn by touching.

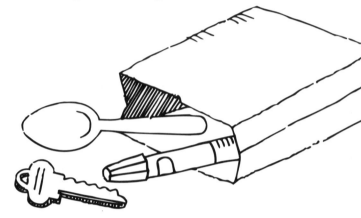

A Touch Poster

Go on a touch hunt around your home. Find things that have different textures:

napkin   yarn

eraser   sand paper

cotton ball   cork

plastic   burlap

Tape some of the things you find onto paper. Use words like **smooth, soft, rough,** and **scratchy** to tell how each thing on your poster feels.

A Touch Bag

Here's a game you can play with a friend:

- Put five small items into a brown paper bag. Don't let anyone see what you put into the bag.

- Ask someone to close his or her eyes and touch an item in the bag. The person then tries to guess what the item is by feeling it.

- Play the game again. This time, the other person can put items into the bag, and you can guess.

You and your child can make a *Please Touch* book to tell about different textures. Paste samples, one to a page, and write sentences for them: *Cotton is soft* or *Sand is gritty.* Then staple the pages together.

N is for Nap

N n

Color the pictures that begin with n. Then practice writing Nn next to those pictures.

Picture Names: *nurse, needle, yarn, necklace, napkins, fork*

Sliding Words

Remember how many different things your hands can do? Well, here's something special you can do with the word **hand**.

Sliding Word Cards

The word **hand** is part of the word family **and**. You can change the first letter in **hand** to read and write new words. One way to change the first letter is to make a sliding word card. Here's how:

- Use the word card and letter strip on page 91 as a pattern. Trace it onto another sheet of paper and cut it out.

- Have a grownup cut along the dotted lines to make two slits.

- Then trace and cut out the letter strip.

- Pull the letter strip through the slits on the word card.

- As a letter appears in the window, read the new word!

Now try making a sliding word card for **hot** and the words in the **ot** family. What other word families can you make sliding word cards for?

Your child can construct his or her own sliding word cards to practice other phonograms, such as *-at*, *-ug*, *-it*, and *-et*.

Two Sliding Words

You can trace these patterns to make sliding word cards.

```
------
_____ and
```

```
------
_____ ot
```

b
h
l
s

(for -and)

d
g
h
l
n
p

(for -ot)

Books to Share

Many picture books, both fiction and nonfiction, deal with emotions and the five senses. Below are four titles that you might choose from.

Feelings by Joanne Brisson Murphy (Aladdin, 1989). A boy expresses his feelings throughout the day and in different situations. Talk about how your child might feel in similar situations.

The Grouchy Ladybug by Eric Carle (Crowell, 1977). A grouchy ladybug, who challenges everyone she meets, regardless of size or strength, is finally humbled.

My Five Senses by Aliki (Harper, 1991). This illustrated book clearly and concisely introduces the senses, what each does, and how several are often used together.

This Is the Bear and the Scary Night by Sarah Hayes (Little, Brown, 1993). A stuffed bear is left in the park and spends a scary night alone. A good book for discussing nighttime fears.

More books you might enjoy:

Feeling Things by Allan Fowler (Childrens, 1991). Simple questions and lively illustrations invite children to think about who they are.

Make a Face: A Book with a Mirror by Henry and Amy Schwartz (Scholastic, 1994). Children show emotions with their faces. The mirror lets readers do the same.

My Best Friend by Pat Hutchins (Greenwillow, 1993). A little girl whose best friend can do everything better than she can proves her own worth.

What's the Matter with Carruthers? by James Marshall (Houghton, 1972). Carruthers' friends are worried because the normally friendly bear is acting grumpy and tired.

 Suggestions

Preview the title and pictures on the next page with your child. Ask what he or she thinks the main idea of the story is. Then read it together. Encourage your child to use picture clues and his or her own experiences to determine the feeling words.

✱ To finish the story, your child can draw and write about another animal's feelings or about his or her own feelings.

How I Feel

Panda said, "I feel happy."

Cat said, "I feel sad."

Mouse said, "I feel scared."

Turtle said, "I feel proud."

_____ said, "I feel _____."

Rhyme Me a Story

CHAPTER 6

Three Little Kittens

Three little kittens,
They lost their mittens,
And they began to cry,
   Oh, Mother dear,
   We sadly fear
   Our mittens we have lost.

What! Lost your mittens,
You naughty kittens!
Then you shall have no pie.
   Mee-ow, mee-ow,
   Mee-ow.
No, you shall have no pie.

A Note About Rhyme Me a Story

For many kindergartners, exploring the new is made easier by introducing it through the familiar. For this reason, traditional rhymes and songs are often used to practice rhyming words, letter and sound associations, language patterns, and strategies for reading new or unfamiliar words. The activities in *Rhyme Me a Story* invite children to take a second look at their favorite rhymes and explore these reading skills:

PHONICS/INITIAL CONSONANTS: Our last four initial letter-sound correspondences—*j, r, y,* and *v*—are introduced.

PHONICS/PHONOGRAMS: The phonograms *-et* as in *pet* and *-ut* as in *but* are introduced.

STORY STRUCTURE: Kindergartners learn that stories consist of certain parts, such as characters, setting, and plot. In this chapter, your child will explore the structure of a story to identify the beginning, middle, and end.

Throughout the book, we've introduced reading strategies that children can use to better understand and enjoy what they read. The sixth and final strategy is to *self-question*. In addition to asking their own questions about a story, readers incorporate and use the other strategies. Here's a sampling of the kinds of questions a reader might ask to:

- **make predictions:** What will this story be about? What will happen next? How do I think the story will end?
- **think about words:** Can letter sounds or picture clues help me read this word? Can the sense of the sentence help me?
- **monitor:** Do I understand what I am reading? What can I do to help me understand?
- **evaluate:** How do I feel about what I've read? Do I agree with the actions of the characters?
- **summarize:** Who are the characters of the story? What happened in the beginning, in the middle, and at the end?

Favorite Rhymes

Poems like "Three Little Kittens" are called nursery rhymes. These rhymes have been around for many, many years. In fact, most grownups enjoyed the same, or similar, rhymes when they were children.

🕐 List of Rhymes

With a grownup, take turns reciting nursery rhymes. List the different rhymes you know. The first lines of these familiar rhymes can start you off. If you can say the whole rhyme, add it to your list. Which rhymes are your favorites?

- Mary had a little _____.

- Humpty Dumpty sat on a _____.

    - Little Boy Blue come blow your _____.

    - Twinkle, twinkle, little _____.

    - There was an old lady who lived in a _____.

🌓 Rhyme Collection

Begin a collection of your favorite rhymes. Copy rhymes you like onto paper. Then draw a picture to go with each one. Keep the rhymes in a folder, or put them in a three-ring binder to create a book.

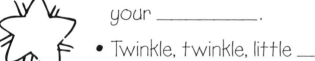

💡 Share with your child rhymes and poems that reflect your family's heritage. You might ask other family members to contribute. Add the rhymes to the collection.

✋ Begin the Rhyme Collection with poems your child already knows and enjoys. Photocopy or print the rhymes so they are easy to read.

Picture This!

Here's an idea you can use to create a poster rhyme for your bedroom wall.

A Rebus Rhyme

Look at "Hey, Diddle, Diddle" on page 99. What do you notice about it? That's right. The rhyme has both words and pictures. It's a rebus rhyme. Try reading "Hey, Diddle, Diddle." Do the pictures help you to read the rhyme?

Labeled rebus pictures like those on page 99 help children make the connection between the printed and spoken word. Consider incorporating rebus drawings into printed materials you might share with your child such as notes, shopping lists, or job charts.

The pencil page that follows is a rebus rhyme your child can color and add to the Rhyme Collection. If your youngster is interested, help him or her create additional rebus rhymes for the collection.

Some kids like silly rhymes. Some prefer animal rhymes. Which do you like better? You can use words and pictures to turn your favorite rhyme into a poster. Here's what to do:

1) Choose a rhyme. How about "Hickory, Dickory, Dock"? Or, a counting rhyme like "One, Two, Buckle My Shoe"?

2) Find words in the rhyme that you can show as pictures. Draw the pictures on a piece of paper and cut them out.

3) Then copy the rhyme onto drawing paper or poster board. Each time you come to a picture word, paste that picture into the rhyme. Hang up your poster!

A Picture Poem

Hey, Diddle, Diddle

Hey, diddle, diddle,

The  cat and the fiddle,

The cow jumped over the moon.

The little dog laughed to see such sport,

And the dish ran away with the spoon.

Rhymes for Outside Fun

Some rhymes are more fun if said while jumping rope or bouncing a ball.

Bouncing Ball Rhymes

Here's a rhyme that also practices a letter of the alphabet. Try bouncing a ball while you say the words.

> J, my name is **Joanie**.
> And my husband's name is **Jack**.
> We live in **Jamestown**.
> And we sell **jelly**.

What letter does this rhyme practice? What words can you use to practice the first letter of your name?

Jump Rope Rhymes

Try jumping rope as you say this rhyme. If you have two people who can turn the rope for you, try to do some of the teddy bear's tricks while you jump.

> Teddy bear, teddy bear
>   Turn around.
> Teddy bear, teddy bear,
>   Touch the ground.
> Teddy bear, teddy bear
>   Turn out the light.
> Teddy bear, teddy bear,
>   Say good night.

Do you know any other jumping rhymes? Perhaps a grownup knows a rhyme he or she could teach you.

Action rhymes passed along orally often vary. "Teddy Bear" is no exception. If it sounds familiar but you can't place it, try substituting *ladybug*, *butterfly*, or *Buster Brown*. Now, which closing lines do you recognize?

- Teddy bear, teddy bear, tie your shoe
  Teddy bear, teddy bear, SKIDOO

- Teddy bear, teddy bear, tie your shoe
  Teddy bear, teddy bear, how old are you? 1, 2, 3, …

- Teddy bear, teddy bear, tie your shoe
  Teddy bear, teddy bear, who loves you? A, B, C, …

J is for Jump

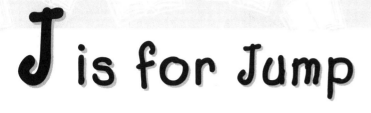

Color the pictures that begin with **j**. Then practice writing **Jj** next to those pictures.

Jj

_____

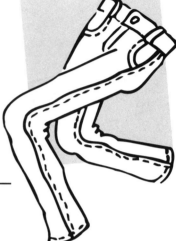
_____

_____

_____

_____

_____

Picture Names: *jar, jeans, jet, jacket, jeep, belt*

Comic Strip Rhymes

You know that some stories and rhymes are long and some are short. But did you know that a rhyme could also tell a story?

⏰ A Story in a Rhyme

Here are the first lines of a few rhymes that tell stories.

Humpty Dumpty sat on a wall ...

The Itsy Bitsy Spider went up the waterspout...

Yankee Doodle came to town ...

Little Bo Peep has lost her sheep ...

Old Mother Hubbard went to the cupboard ...

Now look at the pictures on this page. What nursery rhyme do they show? Yes, "Humpty Dumpty."

You can draw a comic strip like this one to share a rhyme. First, choose a rhyme that tells a story. Then draw the story in three pictures: one for the beginning, one for the middle, and one for the end. Say the rhyme as you share the pictures.

Look in a newspaper with your youngster for comic strips that tell short stories. Talk about the story's beginning, middle, and end.

 Invite your child to include a comic strip rhyme in the Rhyme Collection.

R is for Rabbit

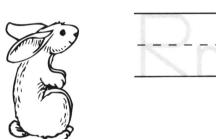

Trace **Rr**. Color the pictures that begin with **r**. Then draw a line to help the rabbit follow the **r** words to the end of the maze.

The End

Picture Names: *rabbit, paintbrush, ring, rope, rooster, rake, table, belt, mouse, hose*

This Is the Way...

We can do a lot of things with rhymes. We can tell stories with them. We can use them to play games. We can sing them. Read on to find out how you can do all three at once!

The Mulberry Bush

"The Mulberry Bush" is a story, a game, and a song. For the first verse, children hold hands, sing, and "go round the mulberry bush." For the other verses, they sing and act out a story:

This is the way we wash the clothes,

Wash the clothes, wash the clothes.

This is the way we wash the clothes,

So early in the morning.

The best part about "The Mulberry Bush" is that you can change the words. Try it. Sing the song as you create your favorite dessert. Here are some ideas:

This is the way I scoop the
 ice cream ...

This is the way I dribble the sauce ...

This is the way I sprinkle the nuts ...

What dessert is this song about?

Improvise your own versions of "The Mulberry Bush" to brighten up any task around the house: setting the table, picking up toys, getting dressed.

Y is for Yellow

_____
Y y

Color yellow the pictures that begin with **y**. Then practice writing **Yy** next to those pictures.

Picture Names: _yo-yo, yak, bike, yawn, yarn, tiger_

105

Act Out a Rhyme

Have you ever tried acting out a story or a rhyme? Here are two ideas.

 ## Put on a Show

Pick a rhyme to act out. How about "Three Little Kittens"? Then gather the props you'll need. Next, practice how you'll act out the rhyme with another person. After a few practices, perform the rhyme for an audience of friends or family members.

 ## Say It with Puppets

Sock puppets can be great projects for rainy days! You can create any kind of puppet you'd like. Here are a few ideas:

- Buttons or snaps make nice puppet eyes.

- Yarn or string can be used for hairstyles.

- Bits of fabric are good for the mouth and things you might want your puppet to wear like a hat, a bow, or a tie.

Once you've created your puppet, slip it onto your hand. Open and close your hand to make it look as though the puppet is talking while you say a rhyme.

V is for Vase

What's hiding? Color each space with a picture that begins with v. What v picture did you find?

Picture Names: *basket, plane, vine, sink, violin, van, belt, buttons, vest, piano*

107

Flip Books

Many rhymes tell stories such as:

I saw a little nut
sleeping in a hut.

To create your own rhyme, you'll first need to find some rhyming words.

Find a Rhyme

You can create flip books to help you find rhyming words. Here's how:

1) Trace the pattern on the next page. Cut out a paper strip for **et**. Then make squares for the letters shown.

2) Put different letters squares in front of **et** to find new words. Save the letters that make real words.

3) Stack and staple the letters you saved onto the **et** strip to make a book.

4) Flip, or turn, the letters to read the words.

Can you use the rhyming words in the **et** flip book to write a rhyme about a **pet**? Try making a flip book for **ut**. What rhyming words did you discover?

Your child may enjoy making flip books for the other phonograms introduced in this book, or he or she may choose another word family to work with.

It might be easiest to photocopy the pencil page that follows to make flip books.

Flip Book Patterns

You can trace and cut out these letter squares to make flip books for **et** and **ut**.

b	g	h	j
l	m	n	p
r	s	v	w

___ e t

___ u t

109

Look at all the things I can do!

☐ I can say and write the letters of the alphabet.

☐ I can name the five senses: see, hear, smell, taste, and touch.

☐ I can name words that begin with the letters c, f, j, k, l, n, p, r, t, v, w, and y.

☐ I can name the letter that stands for the sound at the beginning of words.

☐ I can read words that end with **ig, it, and, ot, et,** and **ut.**

☐ I can tell about the characters in a story.

☐ I can tell what happens at the beginning, in the middle, and at the end of a story.

☐ I can tell if a story is real or make-believe.

☐ I can tell the main idea of a story.

☐ I can tell that some things in a story can cause other things to happen.

Books to Share

You won't have any trouble finding books about rhymes in libraries or in bookstores. Here are some titles— old and new— you might want to share with your child.

Over in the Meadow by Olive Wadsworth (Scholastic, 1985). This classic counting rhyme features animal mothers and their young. Invite your child to chime in on the refrain and verify the numbers.

Oh, A-Hunting We Will Go by John Langstaff (Macmillan, 1974). Rhyming verse and clear illustrations work hand in hand to help beginning readers successfully read the text.

The Cake That Mack Ate by Rose Robart (Kids Can Press, 1986). The cumulative text and rhyming verse, reminiscent of "The House That Jack Built," tells about the cake that Mack ate and where it came from.

The Missing Tarts by B. G. Hennessy (Viking, 1989). See how many nursery rhyme characters you and your youngster can identify as you help the Queen of Hearts find her missing tarts.

More books you might enjoy:

The Complete Mother Goose selected by Ellen S. Shapiro and illustrated by Ethel F. Betts (Random, 1988). All the Mother Goose rhymes you knew as a child—and more.

Poems for the Very Young selected by Michael Rosen and illustrated by Bob Graham (Kingfisher, 1993). A collection of modern and traditional poems from around the world.

Read-Aloud Rhymes for the Very Young selected by Jack Prelutsky and illustrated by Marc Brown (Knopf, 1986). Over 200 short poems suitable for young children.

Sing a Song of Popcorn: Every Child's Book of Poems introduction by Beatrice Schenk de Regniers (Scholastic 1988). Nine Caldecott Medal artists illustrate this collection of 128 well-known poems.

*My Story Suggestions

Read the title aloud with your child and look at the pictures on the next page. Ask your child to predict what this story is about. Then read the story together, helping your child use what he or she knows about the phonogram *-et* to read the rhyming words.

✳ Invite your child to complete the story any way he or she wishes, with or without a rhyming phrase (e.g., *wet)*. After completing the story, ask your youngster to read it to you.

A Little Rhyme

Pat and Tim took out a net.

Tim said, "Watch me get a pet."

Pat said, "No, Tim. Not yet!"

What did Tim and Pat get?

Tim and Pat got _____.